LIFE-CYCLE CELEBRATIONS FOR WOMEN

LIFE~CYCLE

Celebrations

for Women

Marge Sears

Illustrations by Judy Brauch

XXIII

TWENTY-THIRD PUBLICATIONS

Mystic, Connecticut

Twenty-Third Publications
185 Willow Street
P.O. Box 180
Mystic, CT 06355
(203) 536-2611

ISBN 0-89622-399-x
Library of Congress Catalog Card No. 89-50564

Contents

LIFE-CYCLE CELEBRATIONS FOR WOMEN

Introduction

Women today live in a time of transition, weaving together the past and the "not yet." Our consciousness has been raised to question, even to reject, patriarchal structure and worship, but we have yet to fully integrate our women's experience into our spirituality, much less into the religious institutions to which we may or may not still belong.

Our experience as women is fresh with wonder and energy. Through the sharing of personal stories with friends, in small groups of women who share their struggles and triumphs, and in large national women's conferences, some women have come to know their own creativity, wisdom, bondedness, and power. Besides the sharing of personal and communal memories, what is there about women's experience that helps us to define our spirituality?

Women are attentive to their inner voice and cultivate that attention through reflection, meditation, imagery, and other right-brain processes that help to tap their imaginative powers. After centuries of dualistic thinking taught by patriarchal institutions, women are claiming their bodies and using them in exercise, body movement, dance, and in a more sensory prayer and ritual that enhances the whole person. Women are reclaiming universal and natural symbols from tradition that stimulate the senses while promoting mystery by pointing beyond to the sacred. This wholeness of women's experience integrates body, affect, and intellect. On both a personal and communal level, claiming our womanly experience has freed and empowered women to relate to each other in a spirit of inclusivity and sisterhood. This inclusivity extends beyond to the physical world and to all living creation with a caring commitment and a sense of connectedness.

Women today hunger for rituals based on their experience. They listen for inclusive language, look for images that stimulate the senses, and long for songs that sing their everyday experience. They also search for rituals that evoke a deeper meaning; that savor significant life events and passages; that energize them to change and transformation; that build a mutual trust and acceptance; and that celebrate the wholeness of humanity. How do women express this women's spirituality in most of today's Christian churches where one is constantly bombarded by hierarchical structures, exclusion from ministry, sexist language, mistrust of the body, emphasis on past tradition, and meaningless symbols? Many women do not find what they are looking for there. More and more, they opt for or supplement their church worship with prayer and rituals celebrated in small groups and, sometimes, in larger gatherings of women where their needs and interests are accepted and encouraged.

This book is meant to be a resource for those groups and gatherings. Women have every right to weave their colorful threads of experience into the tapestry of today's worship and spirituality. Underlying the rituals included here are many of the principles mentioned above: inclusivity in language and participation; universal images and symbols; shared leadership; use of texts from the Christian tradition *and* elsewhere that give life; and a variety of expressions of prayer that appreciate the whole person. These rituals have been designed for small interactive groups. Breathe your own life into them. Feel free to make additions, deletions, and adaptations to suit your group's needs and experience. Do consider the past worship experience of the group and their comfort level when planning to use any of these rituals. The sharing and celebrating of your stories is more powerful than any form of ritual that you might use to elicit them.

Because our experience is so tied to our bodies and to nature, it is natural that the circle is an important image in women's poetry, literature, art, and ritual. You will find circles from nature—the lunar cycle, mother earth, the cycle of seasons, the cycle of the sun, and the tide cycle—as strong images. More important, the circles we experience through our bodies provide even stronger images: the menstrual cycle, life cycle, even the roundness of our bodies. Women have always been circular (inclusive) in the whole spectrum of their relationships:

- with family, friends, and influential people from the past;
- with different cultures;
- with nature.

These images are part of us and we seek to give them voice in our personal prayer and communal worship.

I have chosen the theme, "Celebrating Full Circle," to help us to enflesh those images in ritual: the cycles of the body, the life cycle, and the circles of relationship. The first section will celebrate those peak changes in a woman's body that in the past may have been degraded or trivialized, but for which women find great significance and satisfaction: pregnancy, childbirth, nursing, menstruation, loss of a child, menopause, and impending death. The second section celebrates social/role transitions through the life cycle: mother/daughter roles; teen/mother reconciliation, mid-life transitions (divorce, empty nest, move, new job); the superwoman syndrome (nourishing yourself), and aging (celebration of the wise woman). In the last section, there are rituals for our circles of relationships: casting a circle of support, empowerment circle, circle of friends, connecting with the past; connecting with the earth and connecting in a global circle.

My hope is that your will find yourself in many of these rituals and that you will share them with your circles of loved ones as together we come full circle in sharing our women's spirituality.

PART ONE

The Cycles of the Body

Celebration of Pregnancy

SYMBOL: Seed

PREPARATION:

Group can gather in a circle with new mother in center. A small basket of seeds (wildflower, vegetable, herb, etc., single or mixed—select according to season or parents' choice) and any type planter with soil (which can be given to child at birth) is placed on the table of celebration.

OPENING:

(Father [or another appropriate support person, i.e., Lamaze coach, best friend] enters circle carrying basket of seeds to stand next to new mother.) From ancient times, people have drawn the connection between seeds sown in the earth and the joining of egg and sperm which is planted in the womb. Seeds are a symbol of

fertility that retain an element of mystery and wonder as well as life-giving power. This mystery and power is shared by females and males. Today, we celebrate the mystery and power of the seed that we all possess but, in a special way, the new life that *(name of mother)* and I have begun. As this basket is passed around the circle, finger the seeds and reflect on the ways that you bring life to others and the world.

(Basket of seeds is now passed from person to person. Appropriate instrumental music, i.e., lullabies, Vivaldi's *Four Seasons*, could be played here.)

RESPONSE:
"Now Is the Season of the Seed"
(A choral reading adapted from a text by an unknown author)

RIGHT SIDE:
Now is the season of the seed. Seed is always the beginning; the seed is small, insignificant, useless in itself. It needs earth, warmth, water, darkness, before the light.

LEFT SIDE:
Now is the season of the seed, the season of the seed falling on the woman, the season of the seed of the world's life hidden in the dark confines of the woman's womb.

RIGHT SIDE:
Drawing life from her the seed will grow. The new life will be formed from the simplicity of the woman's daily life. From her humanity, new humanity takes shape. The seed gives way to shape, to movement, to body.

LEFT SIDE:
She nourishes the body, she nourishes the new person, as Mary nourished Jesus.

RIGHT SIDE:
Now is the season of the secret—the secret of the silent hidden growth of the seed. She continues to be a woman—strong, faithful, loving. Nothing has changed, yet all has been transformed by the seed's coming to be.

LEFT SIDE:
Now is the season of the seed. No less for us than for the woman of Nazareth.

RIGHT SIDE:
Now is the season for the seed of the world's life to find a place of growth and nourishment. Our daily life gives shape, movement, voice, eyes, ears, feet,

hands, humanity to the spirit of the Giver of all gifts.

LEFT SIDE:

Now is the season of the secret, the secret that new life is transforming our lives. It is not shape, movement, body, person that is within the dark confines of ourselves, but it is the Mysterious Creator unfolding in life's experiences, treasuring the discovery of a new self in each of us, gentling our own living with the touch only the Wondrous One gives.

RIGHT SIDE:

Now is our always season, for we are always becoming, always waiting, always treasuring up. Our life is the season, our life is the seed. Full of new beginnings, our life is secret—known only in the dark confines of our inner being.

READER 1: John 1:1, 4, 14

MOTHER:

In the beginning was the seed, in the beginning was the egg that teemed with life. The fertilized egg grew and expanded, full of God's power and mystery, yet dependent on the womb, the mother, for nourishment and shelter. Together, they lived in harmony, taking only what each needed. Through the mother, the child becomes conscious of all of life—its rhythms, music, emotions. So it is with all of us. We are called to nourish and protect the seeds of life we bear and birth. For you and I bear a promise of goodness and harmony. Just as our child will come to us innocent of evil and a bearer of the original harmony of all living beings, so we each gift the world in our own unique way with some goodness that brings harmony. Our child is a promised child, a child with the seed of hope.

SOWING THE SEEDS OF HOPE:

You are invited to share your hopes for this child, for this world, and to pledge your gift to help to bring them about. (*As each person pledges, a seed is taken from the basket and planted in the planter.*)

BLESSING PRAYER:

(*All*) O God, Mother and Father of all creation, we ask a blessing upon these parents who have brought forth the marvelous miracle of life which (*mother's name*) bears in her body, as the earth bears the sown seed.

We rejoice in this miracle and pray for the child alive within her, who will soon join us in the light of day.

May the child's parents find the strength and support to carry and protect this child until that hidden time, when it will break into the world, surrounded by the sunshine of love, and nourished by showers of joy and affection. May this child be healthy of mind and body, unique and beautiful as the first blossom of spring.

May the blessing of the Compassionate One be upon you and your child, a seed of hope for us all.

(Members are invited to lay hands on the mother, sign her with the cross, or greet the new parents with warmth and affection.)

CLOSING SONG:
"Child of Our Dreams" by Marty Haugen, on *Night of Silence*, G.I.A. Publications, Inc.; "Sister" by Chris Williamson, on *The Changer and the Changed*, Olivia Records.

Note: This celebration can also be used for Advent ritual.

Celebration of a Newborn

SYMBOLS: Large candle, Loaf of bread, Time box

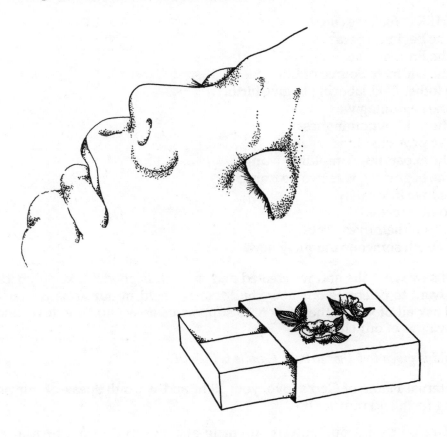

PREPARATION:
Participants are asked ahead of time to bring written wish/blessing for the child that may be shared during celebration, then placed into time box (decorated box, i.e., wooden matchbox, with tight-fitting lid) to be opened by child at puberty. Godparents (or life parents, friends who will form special relationship with child throughout life) should be chosen and then asked to reflect on what values they hope to see nurtured and how they will support parents in raising this child.

INTRODUCTIONS:
(Parents should welcome celebrants and then introduce godparents [or life parents]. The rest of those gathered may give their names and state what their connection is to the child.)

9

CENTERING SONG:

"Thank You, God" by Miriam Therese Winter, on *WomanSong* (Medical Mission Sisters, 1987), or "Sister" by Chris Williamson, on *The Changer and the Changed*, Olivia Records, or "Song of Baptism" by Carey Landry, North American Liturgy Resources.

MOTHER: *(holding child)*

In the beginning was
   the Eternal One
   the Ultimate Source of Life
   Mother God laboring to give birth.
In the beginning was
   the void of nothingness
   the protected inner space
   the expanding, unfolding womb.
In the beginning was two yearning
   to love intimately
   to fill the void
   to join their lives visibly
   to birth someone uniquely new.

God saw what she and we created and said, "It is good." Like all good things, we want to celebrate our new child that we hold in our arms tenderly today and ask all of you gathered here to support us as we nurture, love, and shape the values of our child.

(Child is given to father to hold. Candle is then lit.)

O Eternal Flame of God's love, your light and warmth speak of our power to bring forth and nurture life.

Inspire us to use our powers to create and not to destroy, to heal and not harm, to free and not to smother, and to cherish the life that has been given us in this beautiful child.

As our child lights this candle on each successive birthday, may she (he) come to know your light and warmth as she (he) grows in our love.

FATHER: *(holding child up high)*

We present to all of you, our son *(daughter), (child's full name)*. (Father explains the names chosen and their meaning—who named for, what these persons represent as models for the new child. Both parents can then briefly share special and meaningful experiences connected with the anticipation and birth of this child.)

GODPARENTS:

You, *(names of parents)*, will be the primary caregivers and conveyors of love and wisdom. Will you share with your child your faith and your stories of wise, spirit-filled people? Will you provide a good home that will offer numerous opportunities to learn and live love, peace, and justice?

PARENTS:
We will.

GODFATHER: *(to child)*
(child's name), I rejoice in the honor of being your godparent and to have you as godchild. You will hold a special place in my heart always. I will be there for you whenever I can be of help or support. I pledge to you....*(Share the values you hope to nourish and how you plan to support the child's parents, place the written slip into the time box, and then bless and kiss the baby.)*

GODMOTHER: *(to child)*
(child's name), I rejoice this day as we celebrate what a great gift you are to all of us. You are a unique and precious person to me. I hope that my life will be an example of faith, hope, and love for you as you grow. I pledge to you... (same as godfather).

SHARING OF WISHES/BLESSINGS:
Each celebrant silently or verbally shares a blessing/wish for the child, then places her written slip in time box. Each may then come forward to kiss or sign the baby.

PARENTS:
From all eternity, God has known your name, *(child's name)*, and has held you as precious. Now so do all of us. We rejoice that this dream of God has become flesh and blood, that you have become our child. We pray that we may always encourage you to be all that you can be. We seal this time box of blessings now, to be opened on your twelfth birthday. Then, you will be beginning a new stage of growth, and will again need our encouragement. *(Father seals box with wax.)* May the blessing of God and all of our love surround you your whole life. *(Parents bless and kiss child.)*

GODMOTHER:
Mindful of how life is passed through family and through those who influence and inspire our lives, let us share in this one loaf of bread a sign of our unity in love and good wishes for *(child's name)*. *(Godmother breaks off piece of bread to eat, then passes it around circle.)*

CLOSING SONG:
"By Name I Have Called You" by Carey Landry, N.A.L.R, or any appropriate song of parents' choice.

Note: The celebration can be used as a pre- or post-baptismal celebration.

Healing Ritual
Following Stillbirth or Miscarriage

SYMBOL: Memorial plant or tree

PREPARATIONS:

Prior to ritual, mementos of expected child (ultrasound pictures, prenatal vitamins, maternity clothes, baby clothes and items, etc.) should be gathered. Table large enough to hold mementos plus plant is placed at one end of the room and a storage trunk or box is placed at the opposite end of the room.

PARTICIPANTS:

Mother, father, and any family members or friends who were supportive to parents during pregnancy and time of crises.

SONG:

"Isaiah 49" by Carey Landry, from North American Liturgy Resources (N.A.L.R.).

PRAYER FROM THE COMMUNITY:

O Great Mother/Father God, power over all life, we come to this day with heavy hearts. These parents, *(names of parents)*, were expecting a child into their lives. They had already begun to prepare and plan for this new life in their home. The young life that had begun to grow and develop was quietly and mysteriously ended. They are left now with a void in their home, in their arms, and in their hearts. A part of their very own lives has died. We are saddened by the insufficient virility of so fragile a beginning. We are angry that a life that held so much expectation and hope is now gone. We are helpless to know why this joyous beginning could not come to fullness.

Join us in our tears and sorrow at the loss of this beloved child, *(name of child)*, who has been taken from these parents. As they longed to hold their child close, embrace now this child close to your heart forever.

PARENTS' SHARING:
(Parents can speak what is in their hearts—what the pregnancy meant to them [excitement, anticipation, hopes and joys, worries, anxieties], the events leading up to the stillbirth or miscarriage [pain, waiting, fear, leaning on one another, etc.], last words to the child [how they wanted him or her, their love, and desire to remember], and the need for support now from those gathered. Tears will come, so take as much time as you need.)

READING:
Jeremiah 1:4-8, Luke 18:15-17

INTERCESSIONS:
You may now offer prayers from the heart (for the parents, for the child, for others who experience loss, for those close to child, etc.). Each intercession is followed by all praying: God of Compassion, hear us.

STORING OF MEMENTOS:
(In silence, parents place the mementos in the trunk or box slowly and reverently. Then the lid is closed.)

PRAYER:
Help us, God of Life and Death, to go on. Support us as we struggle to affirm life in the people who depend on us. Heal *(parents' names)* of their sorrow and make them whole. Help us to lift them up, wrap them in our love, and share our energy with them as they try to gather their lives again and continue bringing life to the world. We will offer our support in time of need. *(All repeat.)*

PLANTING OF LIVING MEMORIAL:
(If weather permits, process outdoors with plant or tree to place in soil. A slip of biodegradable paper with the child's name on it is planted among the roots in the earth [or in the planter if indoors] by the parents. Parents explain why this type of plant or tree was chosen and how it will be a reminder of their child.)

(Then all say:) As this plant grows and absorbs this slip of paper, so, too, will the love and memory of this child grow in our hearts.

GREETING OF PEACE: *(A sharing of hugs and kisses)*

CLOSING SONG:
"He's Got the Whole World," traditional spiritual, use appropriate verses. ("She" may be substituted for "He."), or "Bloom Where You Are Planted" by Carey Landry, N.A.L.R., or "You Are Near" by Dan Schutte, S.J., on *Neither Silver or Gold*, N.A.L.R.

Ritual for
A Nursing Mother and Child

SYMBOL: Milk and honey

PREPARATION:
   A rocker (if possible) will be part of the circle for the nursing mother and child.
   A small table is in the center with flowers (to be given to the new mother after
   the ritual) and space for the symbols (empty goblet, small pitcher of milk, and
   small dish of honey).

CENTERING MUSIC:
   "Mother and God" by Miriam Therese Winter, on *WomanSong* (Medical Mission Sisters, 1987), or instrumental Ave Maria, or "Joy" by George Winston.

(Well into song, symbols are brought to the circle one by one, lifted up high; followed by mother and child.)

SPEAKER 1:
There is something sacred about a woman's capacity to nurse.

SPEAKER 2:
If she is receptive, her body will offer her its own special grace.

SPEAKER 3:
We are vessels, grounds of being, from whom flows maternal love.

ALL:
Blessed is the womb that bore us, and the breasts that nursed us! (Luke 11:27)

REFLECTION:
(In darkened room, show slides of mothers and children including celebrants and/or artworks of madonna and child. Or, spotlight picture of mother and child, or madonna and child, with instrumental music [lullaby]).

BODY AWARENESS EXERCISE:
(Lower lights if possible. Play some tranquil instrumental music faintly.)

Stand and close your eyes.
Become aware of all the sensations in your body.
Position your body as if it were a vessel of some sort. *(Hold.)*
    What are you opening up to?
    What will fill you?
Now, position your body as that vessel pouring out. *(Hold.)*
    What is pouring out of you?
    How? In a trickle? flow? torrent?
Now, sit and position yourself as if holding a sucking child. *(Hold.)*
    Who/what are you holding?
    How are you being touched?
    What parts of your body are involved?
    How do you feel connected?

SHARING:
(The empty vessel is passed around the circle. As each woman receives it, beginning with the nursing mother, share a reflection on the body exercise or own experience of nursing [or not nursing].)

SHARING MILK AND HONEY:

LEADER:
Let us celebrate the womanly yearning to give, to feed, to connect, to bond, to pour out grace to the world, and to bring sweetness to life, learned through the lessons taught by our bodies.

(Nursing mother reverently pours milk into the goblet. Goblet of milk and dish of honey are raised high for a few moments. Then the cup is passed and shared from person to person. As this is done, say: "Taste and see the goodness of Mother God." Do the same with dish of honey as each person takes a bit of honey on fingertip to taste.)

BLESSING OF MOTHER AND CHILD:
(Bring rocker into center of circle. Mother and child sit while others touch or hold hand over mother and child.)

Eternal Mother God, you who never forgets one of your own,
    bless this mother who carried this child in her womb,
    feeding and protecting her (him) with her own life fluids.

Bless her breasts and the milk that flows out from her total self
    to this burrowing, sucking creature for her (his)
    satisfaction, growth, and fulfillment.

Bless the bond that is being built between them
    in the dark of the night as mother and baby learn
    the needs and inconsistencies of each other's rhythms,
    for this is the primary experience of affection and relationship.

Bless this mother's milk, an agape flowing through the child
    and thence into the universe,
    a communion through effortless participation and giving.
    May this translucent milk be the connective tissue,
    not only between mother and child, but between them and the cosmos.

Nature creates and flows through her,
    a giver of primordial life stuff,
    building human flesh and life on the essence of mother love.

She is blessed. (*All repeat.*)

ALL: "Tribute" by Marge Sears

We honor you, O Universal Mother!
We were born connected, past to future,

Nourished on your warm sweet milk
Flowing like a mighty river
Flooding the earth in one life-giving stream.

At your bosom of life, we are satisfied—
    body and spirit.
Flesh to flesh, we are linked—
    grandmother, mother, daughter—
Drawing from the Ancestral Source.

We honor you, O Universal Mother!
We are one with our origin, Mother God.

CLOSING SONG:
"Peace Is Flowing Like a River" by Carey Landry, on *I Will Never Forget You*,
N.A.L.R.

Additional Verses:
    Her love is flowing...
    Her milk is flowing...
    Her life is flowing...
    Her sweetness is flowing...

Celebration (at the Start) of Menses

SYMBOLS: Red candle, Green candle, Decorated egg

PREPARATION:
   If this celebration is for a young girl at the start of her menses, women whom the girl knows well and has some comfort with, as well as friends, could be invited to participate.

   Matches, candles, and decorative egg (ethnic, hand-decorated, glass, ceramic, etc.) placed on stand or pillow should be on table in center of the circle. Songs should be practiced.

SONG:
   "We Are Gentle, Loving People" by Holly Near. Suggested verses could be "We are life-giving women," "We are strong, creative women," or verses of your own.

INTRODUCTION:
   Even now, the negative myths about a woman's menstrual cycle have marginalized women from sacred powers. In ancient times, menstruating women were looked upon as taboo, kept from worship, and prohibited against touching holy objects. Even today, when we bleed, we are sometimes looked upon as weak and emotional, unable to hold positions of power.

The flow of blood in menstruation is connected to our life-giving powers to conceive and bear children. Native Americans believed that women symbolized the community's highest creative potential during their period. Today we celebrate that great mystery of dying away to make way for new potential, especially for *(name of young woman)*.

READING: "Changing Woman" by Marge Sears

Changing Woman, mother of all.
Bring the seasons—winter to fall.
Mother of nature, birthing the trees—
Spring green sapling to red falling leaves.

A young girl enters your house
As blood begins its course—
A passage to womanhood—
As the moon wanes o'er the woods.

Changing Woman, teach the flow of life—
Red dissolved into green, day into night.
Sing the sacred song to ease her journey
Of the rhythmic monthly dying to new potency.

Changing Woman, cyclicly we return to our source,
We dedicate the fertility of our life force.
We celebrate your saving grace, the transmission
Of creativity, spirit, and intuition.

(Lighting red candle) This red candle represents for us the egg that dies in each monthly cycle and the blood that is sloughed off with it to make way for new life.

SHARING:
(Women share stories of their own transition to womanhood: good and bad experiences, joys and difficulties of menstruation, and how they respect the cycles of their bodies. Young women can express their expectations and hopes in becoming women. Green candle is lit.)

This green candle represents the power of new life, the possibility of an egg being fertilized to create a new child, and the power of creativity in all of us. We claim and take responsibility for our life-giving powers. Let us now bless our bodies as we bless all of creation.

LIFE POWER BLESSING:
(All) O Great Creator, Spirit of the Universe, you bring new life to all things and you recreate and restore energy to the world at every instant. You shower the heavens with stars every night and you show your glory in the rising sun each morning. You display your grandeur in an outburst of spring flowers after a long winter's snows. You make the dying grasses dance and the trees sing with the power of your winds. Each day we see creation anew.

(Lay hands on the young woman or over your abdomen.) Bless this young woman (us), O Mother God, and the potential for life that she (we) bear(s). Wipe away all that would crush life and destroy beauty. Help her (us) to feel your energy and transmit your life-giving power with respect and awe. May she (we) respect her (our) body, especially during menstrual periods, by giving it rest, proper diet, attention to special needs, and time to attend to her (our) innermost self.

PRESENTATION OF EGG:
(if applicable) Mother presents decorated egg to daughter and says a few special words to her about her hopes for the future, which could include a granting of new privileges or responsibilities.

SONG:
"Renew the Earth" by Marsie Sylvestro, on *Circling Free*, Moonsong Productions.

CELEBRATION:
(A sharing of refreshments and conversation would add a festive note.)

Celebration at
The Onset of Menopause

SYMBOL: Fire

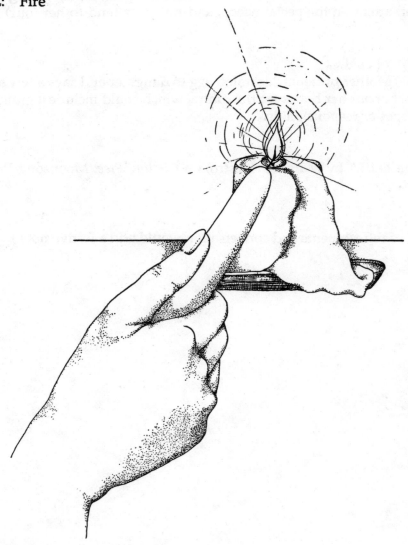

PREPARATION:

On the celebration table, place a red candle in candleholder with matches, paper napkin, and a purple candle placed next to it. Plain tapers given to each participant can be placed on their seats. Table is in front of celebrant's place.

Song should be practiced and the following instructions given for forming the birth arch *(see other option below)*. Two parallel single lines are connected by having opposite pairs of women stretch out their arms and join hands, forming an arch that opens into the circle of celebration. The room could be darkened somewhat.

OPENING:
"Let the Women Be There" by Marsie Sylvestro on *Crossing the Line,* Moonsong Productions.

(Participants are invited to form the birth arch, then the song begins. After first verse, celebrant enters arch and is greeted and hugged by each pair as she passes through and until she enters circle of celebration to stand at her seat by table. Then the arch breaks down, pair by pair, beginning with the pair closest to circle and outward, until all are standing at their seats in the circle. [Another option: Participants are seated and celebrant enters circle, greeting each person.] Red candle is lit and all are invited to reflect on the flame of the red candle, sign of the creative power of our childbearing years.)

JOYS AND REGRETS OF THE PAST:
(Celebrant reflects about her experience of the childbearing years.)

FRIEND OR MENTOR:
(Read this slowly and dramatically.) *(Name)* is here to celebrate the passing of an energy that can birth other human beings and to recognize a fuller type of creative energy, an energy that can create art, music, home, community, knowledge, or a world of justice (add or change to suit interests of celebrant). Although she will no longer ovulate and bleed monthly, she can channel her energy through her whole body, mind, and spirit. Although she will no longer be capable of bringing forth children, she can now bring forth transformation and growth to whatever she touches.

As a sign of that passing away of one energy to another, *(name)* will now light the purple candle, symbol of her new energy, from the red candle of her birthing energy. She will then extinguish the red candle, allowing a few drops of wax to fall away, and will replace it with the candle of new fire. *(Celebrant lights purple candle, etc.)*

SHARING OF A NEW VISION:
(Celebrant shares her hopes and vision of what lies ahead for her as the bearer of life to a broader world.)

ALL:
We rejoice with you as you enter into the greater fullness of your creative power. May the fire of your creativity ignite our world with your light and warmth.

READING: Luke 8:16

PASSING ON THE LIGHT OF CREATIVE POWER:
(Celebrant begins lighting the tapers of the women on either side of her. The flame is passed around the circle until all tapers are lit. Pause a moment in silence.)

ALL:
We rejoice in the light of women's creative energy in all phases of life. May it always shine bright for the world to see.

CLOSING SONG:
Sing again "Let the Women Be There," or "I Am Woman" by Helen Reddy, or song chosen by celebrant.

Comfort Ritual for
An Impending Death

SYMBOL: Fragrant oil

BACKGROUND:

Death and dying in our culture are not easy life passages to talk about, much less ritualize. Yet, in our modern, technical hospitals, a very natural event in our life cycle can be sterile and cold, separate from the people who care for the dying person. Like the women in the Bible, who are present at the cross as well as the tomb, this ritual attempts to surround the dying one with support and personal care whether in the hospital, nursing home, or at home.

Environment means a lot here (fresh flowers, glowing candles, balloons, or favorite music), but the person's wishes should define what happens in the ritu-

---

al. The ritual can have any or all of the following aspects that will help both the dying and those close to them to experience the wide range of emotion that impending death elicits.

PREPARATION:
(On bedside table, there should be a glass or vase of water, a flower, a container of fragrant oil, cotton balls, and a favorite object, i.e., flowers, food, collectible, item from favorite craft or hobby.)

OPENING:
(Some favorite piece of instrumental music plays in the background until all are ready to begin.) We gather together as persons bonded in some way to *(name)* and wanting to give our care and support as she (he) prepares for death. This is not an easy time for any of us, for in facing death, we each face our own mortality. So we come as well to receive her (his) wisdom and perspective, a culmination of life's experience.

RECONCILIATION:
(Dying person can share those aspects of life in which one feels a sense of failure, has left things unfinished, has regrets, or has been dissatisfied. First the person, then the others, are sprinkled with flower dipped in water.)

ALL:
Compassionate God, we seek a way to forgive one another and to find a way to peace and unity. All of our lives are divided by light and darkness, goodness and bad. We embrace all that is hidden in us as we seek to forgive ourselves and let go of guilt and failure.

Our brother Jesus, in your life you inspired us to deal with separations between us and to be one. Heal our hurts and renew the solidarity that can extend beyond this life. Amen.

PASSING ON RESPONSIBILITY AND HOPE:
(Dying person might share concerns about how things will go on if she [he] is not here to complete them, and might share a vision of the future that she [he] will not be able to bring to fulfillment. Then the dying person charges those persons present to carry it on.)

ALL:
O Fullness of Life, how hard we find the letting go. We fear that something, or more important, that we will be forgotten. We hand over our unfinished plans and dreams to those we love and to you, who said you would never forget us. *(Name)*, allow yourself to let go of responsibilities and hopes to others who will treasure them as their own because they are a part of you. Be at peace now.

(Each person takes a turn to anoint some part of the body with fragrant oil. A piece of music could be played here like "I'll Never Forget You" by Carey Landry, N.A.L.R., or "Having Been Touched" by Chris Williamson, on The Changer and the Changed, Olivia Records.

A GATHERING OF GOODNESS:
(Something that has brought the person pleasure in his or her life can now be placed in the person's hands.) Your goodness surrounds us like your hands surround this (object). Think about the good times in your life, the good that you have done, and when you have most felt the goodness of life. *(Pause. Those gathered can briefly share the goodness they have seen in this person's life. When finished, all can join hands to pray:)*

O God of Goodness, who gathers us together as one, you have gifted us with the life of *(name)*. When you take *(name)* back to you, O Source of Life, we will keep the memory of her (him) alive in our hearts. We are grateful for all that we have shared in our times together—work, humor, trust, affection, and celebration. Our lives have been touched and enriched. May she (he) feel our love and support until his (her) last breath, as we continue to keep vigil with her (him). Amen.

(End with a little private time and a hug from each individual, or with music ["On Eagle's Wings" by Michael Joncas, N.A.L.R.], and brief refreshments.)

PART TWO

Celebrations
Around the Life Cycle

Celebration of
Mother and Daughter Bond

SYMBOLS:
Pair of candles, Bowl of rose petals or potpourri, Bell, Small dish of salt, Clear pitcher of water and bowl, Cup of wine.

PREPARATION:
Symbols listed above are set out decoratively on a table large enough to have space for additional mementos (pictures, symbols, heirlooms) of their mothers that participants were instructed ahead of time to bring. Each section (symbol) can be led by a different participant.

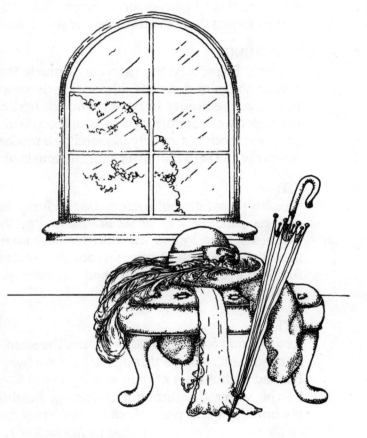

OPENING SONG:
"Mother and God" by Miriam Therese Winter, on *WomanSong* (Medical Mission Sisters, 1987).

CANDLES:
(*Light candles.*) Blessed be the fire that lights these candles with the light of creation, the light that overcame the darkness of the womb. Blessed be those who taught us to see: nature, works of art, the people we love who gift us with insight, the eye of the heart. We pray to our Mother God.

ALL: Based on Jewish Baruch-she-amar
Blessed is she who spoke and the world became.
Blessed is she.
Blessed is she who in the beginning gave birth.
Blessed is she who says and performs.
Blessed is she who declares and fulfills.

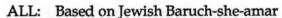

Blessed is she whose womb covers the earth.
Blessed is she who protects all creatures.
Blessed is she who nourished those who are in awe of her.
Blessed is she who lives forever and exists eternally.
Blessed is she who redeems and saves.
Blessed is her name.

ROSE PETALS:

(Toss petals over heads of members.) Blessed is the incense of these flowers. Blessed is the essence of mother nature, of mother earth, of roses, of fresh rain on our mother's garden, of baking bread, and of our mother's cologne. Blessed is the essence that penetrates to our depth and reminds us of home and family.

BELL/CHIME:

(ringing) Blessed be the marvels of music that lullaby us to sleep or sing the simple songs of daily life. Blessed be those who taught us to listen for the joy in music, the beauty in poetry, and the endless sounds of creation. Blessed be the melody of comforting words that soothed a scraped knee, adolescent crisis, or a new mother's anxiety. Blessed be a mother's silence that taught us to open the ear of the soul that listens for the music of the divine voice.

SALT:

(Bowl is passed around circle so that each can take a pinch between their fingers to sprinkle underfoot, then all stand.) Blessed be the salt of the earth, the wise ones before us, who forged the path we now take for granted. Blessed be our feet that walk the path of our foremothers. Blessed be the hands that guided our first and every step, that touched us tenderly, and that let us go to be our own person.

WATER:

(pouring into bowl) Blessed be water, the source of life. Blessed be the waters of our mothers' wombs through which we heard the heartbeat of love and care. Blessed be the tears of pain and joy heard through our growing years. Blessed be the water that brought cleansing, healing, and play. We remember our birthmothers and pray: *(Each woman brings up the memento of her mother to place on the table as she offers a prayer for her mother.)*

WINE:

(Cup of wine is raised.) Blessed be wine, the luscious fruit of the vine. Blessed be our joys in life. Blessed be those that inspire, that stimulate us to be all we are and more. Blessed be those women who are our mother models. For these women we pray: *(Names are said out loud at random.)*

WATER AND WINE:

(A little water is mixed with the wine.) We mix a little water with the wine to rep-

resent temperance, a quality of women's wisdom. It exemplifies a stretching out so that there is more to share, so common with mothers. Blessed be this cup of wine with water, the cup of generosity, given to us by our mothers, to share with one another but to share also with mothers unknown to us for whom we now pray:

ALL: Taken from "A Mother's Day Prayer" by Andrea Baier

We come today, God of children, to thank you for the many kinds of mothers you have given to our world.

We rejoice with the women who feel loved and appreciated and fulfilled in their role of mother.

We ask you to give faith and perseverance to women who question their ability to nurture and guide their children in a world of uncertainty and doubt.

We thank you for mothers who inspire their children to be the best that they can be and to like themselves.

We ask you to comfort mothers who are sad because they lost a child to death, or prison, or drug addiction.

Comfort, too, those children whose mothers are no longer living. Give them happy memories. You promised you would not leave them orphans.

Bless, too, mothers who have the courage to place a child for adoption when they can give their child life, but cannot give a home. Bless these loving women with peace.

God of Inner Peace, there are women who are sad today because they have lost a child to miscarriage or abortion. Help these mothers to forgive themselves or to forgive you. Give them your peace.

Thank you for mothers who overlook our faults.

O Great Comforter, ease the burden of elderly mothers who live in nursing homes or senior citizen apartments or lonely houses, who are forgotten on this day. Or worse, who are forgotten every day.

For mothers whose children are terminally ill, chronically ill, or mentally ill. Bless them with courage and peace. Let them feel your love surrounding them and their children.

For grandmothers, den mothers, godmothers, mothers-in-law, and women with no title who mothered us when we needed it.

Help mothers and children to love each other enough to always tell the truth.

Give us love and patience to always treat each other as human beings.

Help us remember that we are all children of the same Creator, worthy of respect and honor today and every day. Amen.

CLOSING SONG:
"Song of Women" by Carolyn McDade, on *This Tough Spun Web*, Women at Grailville.

Reconciliation Ritual Between Mother and Teen

SYMBOLS: Ashes, Water, Gift

BACKGROUND:
This ritual can be celebrated immediately following a disagreement, hurting words, or impasse in communicating. It can also take place when both parties mutually agree that the time is right to make a new beginning in the relationship. This ritual could be used in many other relationships as well. It is based in part on the Native American sweat lodge ritual with its four main segments: 1) emptying; 2) visioning; 3) asking assistance from a higher being; and 4) sharing appreciation.

PREPARATION:
Participants could take time beforehand to reflect on and write out on a sheet of paper all the images, angry words, and emotions of the relationship in the past. If time allows, the gift to be shared at the close of the ritual could be selected ahead of time. Have handy matches, a can for ashes, pitcher of water, towel, and bowl or basin.

1. EMPTYING:
(Openly share and hear the anger, hurt, and fears that have taken place in the past between you [can be read from paper]. This is an emotional labor that will birth a new relationship. Like contractions, let the angry words, the tears, and the hard emotions come one by one. Take time with each other. When the sharing has been completed to both persons' satisfaction, burn the sheets of paper in silence [into a can]. Mix the ashes together and smear some ash on one another's hands as a sign of each other's willingness to carry each other's weaknesses.)

2. VISIONING:
(Share images and hopes of what the relationship could be. When sharing is completed to satisfaction of both, wash and dry each others' hands with gentleness and care as a sign of mutual forgiveness. We wash away the old ways to begin something new.)

3. PRAYER TO A HIGHER BEING:
(Each takes a turn to pray for the strength, energy, and power of love to grow into this new relationship. You might bring to the prayer names of those who have modeled the qualities of relationship that you envision. Then pray together:)

O Compassionate One, we come together as we seek to forget the past and its mistakes and to be united in love in a new relationship.

We have forgiven each another for the pain we have caused each other, now help us to heal the hurt of our actions and words.

Fill us with your healing power, O Gentle One, so that we might come to each another with new respect, greater freedom, and renewed love.

BOW OF HONOR (optional):
(Based on the Japanese expression of respect and honor, stand and face one another with folded hands. Bow to each other slowly and reverently. The mother then covers the hands of her teen with her own and bows again. She releases them, folds her hands, and bows again. There is a period of silence. Each bows reverently to the other. The teen covers the mother's

hands with her own and bows. Then she releases her hands, folds them, and bows to the mother. Then each bows reverently to the other. This section can be completed by sharing a hug.)

4. AFFIRMATION:

(While holding hands, fill the spaces emptied of anger and hurt with words of love, words about what you find lovable in each other.)

5. GIFTING:

(Each should give something to the other that is precious or especially meaningful [i.e., an article of clothing the other has always admired, a family heirloom, something you created, something of sentimental value]. Continue to celebrate in a manner agreeable to both people.)

Celebration of Entry
Into Full Adulthood
Mid-Life

SYMBOL: Mirror

PARTICIPANTS:
People who were crucial during the earlier life of celebrant could be invited. If not, pictures of these significant people could be used. Double-faced tape is placed on backs of the pictures.

PREPARATION:
On center of the celebration table, three mirror tiles are placed upright, backs against each other, forming a triangle. Also on table are a hand mirror, pictures, various scented candles, and matches.

OPENING SONG:
"Song of the Soul" by Chris Williamson, on *The Changer and the Changed*, Olivia Records, or "Let It Be" by the Beatles, or lively instrumental music.

INTRODUCTION:
Currently, it is popular to throw "over the hill" parties for people who have reached mid-life. Mid-life is more accurately a middle period, a period of full adulthood, a period of increased inner life tasks, and a period of growth rather than decline. Today we reject the media's youth-oriented image of aging. We celebrate a new level of self-responsibility, of generativity, and of balance. Along with *(name)*, we quest a new vision as we look to the next phase of living.

A LOOK WITH GRATITUDE TO THE PAST:
(Celebrant picks up hand mirror and turns toward person(s) who contributed to who she is to catch their reflection in the mirror. Celebrant acknowledges how they had impact. If a significant person is not present, picture can be tacked to hand mirror and shown to group. Proceed until all are acknowledged.)

READER 1:
In the initial phase of life, who we are was first shaped by our parents, then peers, career, spouse, children, and life circumstances. We were, for the most part, reflections of others.

READER 2:
Now, we must accept and bless ourselves for who we uniquely are. *(One mirror tile is placed down, mirror side up as celebrant stands behind table looking down into mirror.)*

READER 1:
In the initial phase of life, we were absorbed with making our place in the world.

READER 2:
Now, we must focus on what we can give back to the world in gratitude so that we can continue to grow. *(Second tile is placed down next to first tile, mirror side up. Last tile is propped up.)*

READER 1:
In the initial phase of life, we looked to the future—to becoming, to perfecting, and to saving the world.

READER 2:
Now, we seek balance by just being, savoring, synthesizing, and living in the present. *(Third mirror is placed down, mirror side up, adjacent to the other two. Pause.)*

COMMITMENT TO FUTURE GROWTH:
One by one, *(name)* will state the actions and values that she will seek to develop in this next period of her life. She asks that we support her in each commitment by having one person from the group stand after each commitment is shared and say: I will support *(name)* in her commitment to.... *(Then, coming to the table, the person lights one of the candles, placing it on the mirror tiles.)*

(When finished, celebrant says:) You are my witnesses now to these commitments I make toward a new perspective on living as a full adult. As you were

a part of the refining and polishing of the last *(number of years)*, may you continue to illumine me as I reflect your light and love through the prism of my living.

PRAYER:
Eternal God/dess, transcending time, we yearn to know your mystery like Alices who enter the looking glass. Yet our bodies remind us that we are one with creation, susceptible to aging and death, so we redeem its darkness with our vivid rays of light. May we grow in the light of inner wisdom and grace-filled activity, day by day. Amen.

CLOSING SONG:
"This Little Light of Mine," traditional black spiritual, or "You Light Up My Life" by Debby Boone, Warner Records, or a celebrant's favorite.

Celebration of Transition
Divorce, Empty Nest, New Job, Move

SYMBOLS: Large tree branch, Fruit

PREPARATION:
   On a small table is a large bowl or vase of water. A long tree branch lays at its side. Each person is given a piece of fruit before celebration begins. Also on the table is an empty wooden bowl.

CENTERING MUSIC:
   "Autumn" from Vivaldi's *Four Seasons,* or any selection from George Winston's *Autumn* album, Windham Hill Records, or "Fly, Fly, Fly" from Libana, on *A Circle Is Cast,* Spinning Records, (optional: slides of autumn scenes or past scenes of the celebrant's life)

MEMORIES OF THE BEGINNINGS:

(Person undergoing transition dips both hands into water in bowl or vase, lifting cupped hands high so water visibly runs down.) Water is the symbol of birth and beginning. Water surrounds and protects the child in the womb and it swells the acorn to begin life as a tree.

(Take branch and dip end in water and sprinkle those gathered with the water. Branch is left in vase.) Let us recall memories of the many new beginnings in each of our lives. *(Pause.)* As I face a new beginning, I would like to pause to remember the excitement and the goodness of the past (relationship, job, birth of children, home, etc.). After I have shared, please feel free to share any memories you have.

READING: Ecclesiastes 3:1-8

LETTING GO:

There is a time to hold on and a time to let go, a time to link our lives together and a time to sever ties, and a time to begin and a time to end. Rituals like this one help us to let go of our previous experiences so that we can allow ourselves to move on, to be free, to dream again, or to be more wholly ourselves.

(The person can tell her story of transition, naming those aspects that she will leave behind and the feelings associated with them. As each aspect is named, a leaf is pulled off the branch.) Change is not easy. Yet the events of our lives constantly call us to change our ways. It is natural to resist change, because it is often painful and costly. However, only through letting go, like the trees in autumn, can we begin again, grow, and bring forth new fruit.

PRAYER: *(All)*

O Creator, prune the dead and rotting from our spirits,
  the diseased that would further destroy us,
  the parasitic that would cause us to shrink rather than expand.
O God of Beginnings and Endings, prune the barren branches,
  the withering limbs, and the strangling tentacles.
  Free us from the overarching trivia of our lives.
Cut away all that weighs down our lives or retards our creativity—
  Even that part of us that is still green with the sap of life,
  that part of us not yet brittle—remove;
So that new life can sprout, multiplying in abundance,
  bearing fruit beyond our present yield,
  an increase beyond our present vision. Amen.

OFFERING OF FRUITFUL WISHES:

(Vase with branch is raised.) Even a branch, stripped bare of its leaves, becomes

a source of new life as fuel, material for house, chair, or bowl. Let us offer our hopes and good wishes for *(name)* in her new beginning as we fill this wooden bowl with good fruits. (Each person offers a good wish, puts the fruit in the bowl, and hugs the woman in transition. The bowl is lifted high.) We offer these fruits of the future as a sign of our willingness to let go and risk change, trusting and hoping for fuller lives. (All) Amen.

CLOSING SONG:
"A Wonderful Change," traditional black spiritual, or "Turn, Turn, Turn" by the Byrds, on Columbia Records, or "Be Not Afraid" by Bob Dufford, S.J., N.A.L.R.

Superwoman Ritual
Nourishing Self

SYMBOL: Bowl of luscious fruit

PREPARATION:
  Women are requested ahead of time to bring something to the gathering that
  they use to help refresh or renew themselves (bath salts, lotion, hairbrush, music, etc.). Environment should be designed for comfort and relaxation (pillows,
  soft music, candles, fresh flowers, incense or potpourri). A table in the center
  should be large enough to hold items the women bring plus the bowl of fruit.

CENTERING:
"Hipswinging a Safe Road" by Carolyn McDade, on *This Tough Spun Web*, Women at Grailville, or "Waterfall" by Chris Williamson, on *The Changer and the Changed*, Olivia Records, or "Getting Tired Blues" by Marsie Sylvestro, on *Circling Free*, Moonsong Productions.

READING: *(Each person around the circle can take a turn reading a line.)*
1. We are strong women who speak the truth.
2. We are hearty women who love 'til it hurts.
3. We are hardy women who work and clean out the dirt in every nook and cranny of the world.
4. We are virile women not afraid to cry because it opens our eyes to others' pain.
5. We are determined women who seek to do what others determined should or could not be done.
6. But, as women, we are strongly afraid that we cannot do it alone.
7. We are superwomen caught in so many separate battles that we need to pull in our energies, disconnect from others' needs, just to nurture ourselves in body, mind, and soul.

ENERGY MEDITATION:
(Someone leads this meditation, or has it recorded on tape, reading phrase by phrase, leaving time for quiet.) Close your eyes and take a few deep breaths. Be aware of how you are sitting...how you are breathing....Imagine that your breath travels to any place in your body where you want release and that it carries away with it any tension....Let yourself settle into the floor. Feel all the parts of your body. Imagine that a cord runs through the center of your body to support you so that you do not have to make any effort to hold yourself up.

The air cushions you on all sides, giving you comfort and support....Now imagine that each time you inhale you are sending warmth and peace to the part of you that needs healing or relaxing....Feel this energy streaming through your body like warm, soothing water....Feel the connections of all of your parts....

You are a whole, creative person that is connected to the energy flow of the cosmos. Allow its energy to flow through you, energizing, renewing, revitalizing you....When you are ready, touch various parts of your body and feel your energy. Gradually open your eyes.

SHARING OF REFRESHMENTS:
(Each woman brings to the table what she has brought that brings her refreshment and explains it. If the group has unlimited time, the refreshment can be shared with the others. [Brush each other's hair, massage, play the music, etc.]).

CIRCLE OF HANDS MEDITATION:

(Someone again leads as all sit in circle and join hands.) Close your eyes and again be conscious of your breathing as energy flow....Imagine that the breath-energy flows from the hand of the woman on your left into your hand and across your shoulder and out of your right hand to the woman on your right. She passes it along to the next, and next, and so on until it circles around back to you, continuing.

Feel yourself as part of the whole group. You are feeding one another with your collective energy, soothing, healing, and energizing....Notice how different you feel now from when you began the ritual. Visualize how you feel as a result, leaving here, tomorrow, next week. Feel your strength....How will you continue this energy?....When you are ready, slowly open your eyes.

NOURISHING OURSELVES:

(Pass around the bowl of fruit which is now energized by the group. Before the fruit is eaten, a statement of affirmation is made by each woman of what energy is being planted in herself. For example: "With this *[name of fruit]*, I renew my energy to *[type of energy]*. As it becomes part of me, I will feel its energy rising in me." [Each woman feeds herself, or the person next to her.])

PRAYER OF AFFIRMATION: *(All)*

I am woman.
I am ark and womb.
I am grotto at the center of the rose.
I am the core of the apple where tough seeds form.
Praise what is round and open to new life.

We seek to be whole and entire.
We seek healing that brings energy.
We seek one another and our stories.
We seek not to rest but to transform.
Praise what nourishes and brings about growth.

We are blossoms that provide a cornucopia yield.
We are luscious berries sowing a future harvest.
We bloom and bear fruit.
We are women.
Praise what creates and recreates.

CLOSING SONG:

(Concludes with a sharing of hugs) "Today (while the blossoms still cling to the vine)," traditional folk song, by The New Christy Minstrels, Columbia Records, or "I Feel Like Goin' On," traditional spiritual, on *This Tough Spun Web*, by Carolyn McDade, Women at Grailville.

Celebration of a Wise Woman
60th to 75th Birthdays, Retirement

SYMBOL: Venus symbol

PREPARATION:
Copies need to be made of the Venus symbol (♀), large enough to practically cover an 8" x 11" piece of paper. Colored pencils, markers, chalk, pens are also needed for creative expression. A small decorative bowl of salt is on a small table in the celebration circle along with flowers or other decorations to make the table look festive and/or express the woman being celebrated.

GATHERING:

([Instrumental music of celebrant's choosing] Celebrant can lead participants around the circular seating, then into it to be seated. Or, celebrant can go around circle of seated women, greeting each one as the music plays.)

INTRODUCTION:

We gather as members of *(name)*'s circle of friends who are rooted deeply in her earthly years of experience and connected strongly through her in relationships, still open and expanding. We celebrate *(name)* here today as a wise woman, a woman who has turned her years of knowledge and experience into wisdom.

HONORING OF WISE WOMEN OF INFLUENCE:

Let us honor other wise women who have served as resources of wisdom to us. *(Pause for a moment of reflection.)* One by one, let us name out loud and say a little something about the wisdom they brought.

REFLECTION ON A SYMBOL:

(Pass out Venus symbol sheets.) The Venus symbol, the biological symbol for female, was first an astrological symbol for the feminine, defined as "a circle of spirit on the cross of matter." Many times through the centuries, it has been redefined; so today, as women growing in wisdom, let us define for ourselves this symbol for the feminine. Take a few minutes first to reflect on what being a women means to you at this point in your life and then to write or draw it on the Venus symbol on the sheet. *(After everyone seems to be finished, share briefly what people created on their symbol sheet.)*

WISDOM READING:

The Venus symbol has also stood for the highest attribute of God, her wisdom, as relayed in this reading from Wisdom. "Now what Wisdom is, and how she came to be, I shall relate; and I shall hide no secrets from you. Such things as are hidden I learned, and such as are plain; for Wisdom, the artificer of all, taught me.

For in her is a spirit intelligent, holy, unique, manifold, subtle, agile, clear, unstained, certain, not baneful, loving the good, keen, unhampered, beneficent, kindly, firm, secure, tranquil, all-powerful, all-seeing, and pervading all spirits, though they be intelligent, pure and very subtle. For Wisdom is mobile beyond all motion, and she penetrates and pervades all things by reason of her purity. For she is the aura of the might of God and pure effusion of the glory of the Almighty; therefore nought that is sullied enters into her. For she is the refluence of eternal light, the spotless mirror of the power of God, the image of her goodness.

And she, who is one, can do all things and renews everything while herself perduring; and passing into holy souls from age to age, she produces friends of God and prophets. For there is nought God loves, be it not one who dwells with Wisdom. For she is fairer than the sun and surpasses every constellation of the stars. Compared to light, she takes precedence; for that, indeed night supplants, but wickedness prevails not over Wisdom."

WISDOM SHARING:
(Celebrant shares bits of the wisdom she has learned throughout her lifetime as she has grown. She then shares how this wisdom is leading into the future. Slides of the person's life might accompany this, as an optional feature. Then all say: "We celebrate with you the unending wisdom of your life!")

WISDOM BLESSING:
(Celebrant takes the dish of salt and sprinkles a pinch of salt at the feet of each person. Then, with arms outstretched:) Eternal Wisdom, as women of experience, we are the salt of the earth. Our spirits are grounded firmly in our bodies and we plant our feet firmly on the earth. Yet, our past experience has given us a taste for an expanding world, so we strive to make connections with all creation in ever-expanding circles.

Bless these women, as you have blessed me, with a heightened savoring of the many flavors of life with all its depth and mystery. May they know and use their wisdom all the days of their life. (All) Amen.

SONG:
"Blessing Song" by Marsie Sylvestro, on Circling Free, Moonsong Productions, or "Mystery" by Miriam Therese Winter, on WomanSong, or song of celebrant's choosing.

PART THREE

Celebrating Circles of Relationship

Casting a Circle of Support

SYMBOL: Yarn or cord of appropriate color

PREPARATION:
Group should be seated in a circle. Songs should be practiced if unfamiliar to group.

NAMING WHO WE ARE:
(Someone begins by proclaiming or chanting her name, which the group then repeats. She then takes the hand of a woman to one side of her who then chants her own name. The naming continues until the full circle is closed.)

SONG:
"A Circle is Cast" by Libana, from *A Circle Is Cast*, Spinning Records (1986), or "We Are Casting a Woman's Circle," sung to the tune of "Jacob's Ladder," with the words:

"We are casting a woman's circle...sisters all around.
Come now, join us, cast the circle...sisters all around.
All together, form a circle...sisters all around."

CENTERING THE CIRCLE'S ENERGY:
Close your eyes and take a few deep breaths....Notice how you are sitting...how you are breathing....Every breath travels to whatever part of the body needs tension relieved...Let yourself relax as if sitting on and supported by a cushion of air....Concentrate on your hands and the sensations you experience in them....

Imagine your breath-energy flowing out through your hands to the person on your left, across her shoulders and on to the next person, to the next, the next, flowing around the whole circle, through you again, continuing round....Imagine a bright yellow yarn that connects through you to each person in the group through your arms....The energy flows along this yarn bringing energy to whatever part of your body needs it....(*Pause.*)

You are feeding each other with your collective energy as you will with your sharing, in many ways, both in and out of this group. Let it continue to unite you and weave among you. (*Leave quiet time here.*)

CIRCLE SHARING:
(Members are invited to share their need/purpose/reason for becoming part of this circle.)

WEAVING THE CIRCLE'S ENERGY:
(Leader takes ball of yarn or cord and wraps it around the waist of the woman next to her as she states, aloud or in silence, what energy she brings to the circle. The leader then gives that woman the ball so that it continues in like manner until all are bound together. Then the leader says:)

Be aware of how you felt before coming here. Visualize how you will feel/act/be as a result of this ritual once you leave here. Feel your energy. How will you channel this energy later today? tomorrow? later this week? as part of this group? (*Reflect as song plays.*)

SONG:
"I'm a Woman, I'm a Weaver" by Marsie Sylvestro, on *Crossing the Line*, Moonsong Productions, or "This Tough Spun Web" by Carolyn McDade, on *This Tough Spun Web*, Women at Grailville.

PRAYER: (*All*)
Weaver God, we come as separate strands of colorful threads to be woven in and out, over and through each other's lives into a marvelous fabric of some beautiful, mysterious design. At times, we come to this circle loom, weak and frayed, seeking the strength of others to restore the rich texture of our lives.

We sometimes come snarled and in knots looking for deft hands to stretch us so that we can see our pattern more clearly. Mostly, however, we come to celebrate the beauty of the tapestry when we are together and to weave wholeness at your loom.

(Scissors are passed around the circle so that the cord can be cut between each woman. Women tie a section of cord around each other's wrists as a reminder of the energy of the circle.)

CLOSING SONG:
"Sisters, Now Our Meeting Is Over" by Libana, from *A Circle Is Cast*, Spinning Records, or "Weavers of Life" by Marsie Sylvestro, on *Crossing the Line*, Moonsong Productions.

Celebration of Empowerment

SYMBOL: Light

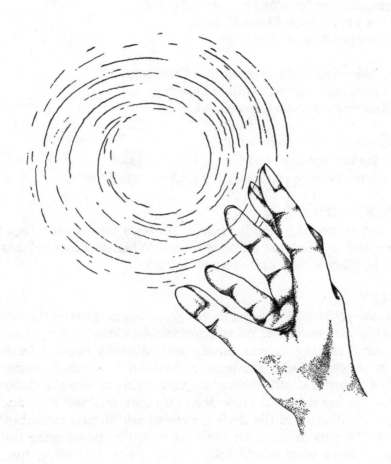

PREPARATION:
Seats are arranged in a circle, allowing enough space in the center to stand and move in a circle. A symbol of energy/light, empowerment is needed (a round glass bowl with votive candle, large candle, a crystal, or whatever seems to represent your group's energy).

GROUP READING: "World of Women" by Marge Sears

(Alternate verses between each half of the circle.)

The world of women is a round world,
  Reaching out horizontally around the earth's curve
    Taking in the world in an embrace.

Wholly round as women's bodies—
  Breasts and hips, bowed as the rocker
in the nursery, gently keeping life's rhythms.

Rounded as smooth pebbles worn by the turbulence
  of stormy seas, yet tornado-like with fury,
cutting swaths for justice's sake.

Women's lives like whorls of leaves around the stem,
  returning to start again, imperceptibly growing,
In an ever-widening cycle over the seasons.

The world of women is a round world.
  On some darkened evening, under an arc of night sky,
    You will see us dancing circles wildly under the full moon.

NAMING OF SELF AND NEED:
(Pass around the symbol of empowerment. As each women receives it, she says her name and a need for empowerment. When the symbol has gone around the circle, place it back on the center table.)

GUIDED IMAGERY:
(Sit in a comfortable position.) We come to this ritual to energize us through celebration, an all too rare occasion. When comfortable, close your eyes and concentrate on your breathing as you slowly and naturally breathe in...breathe out...breathe in peace...breathe out tension...breathe in warmth...breathe out frustration....If a thought is still distracting you, bring it into the darkness at your center and release it there....Look deep into that darkness now and see a sparkle of light, a glimmer of the divine, present within you since birth....As you focus on it, it seems to shimmer with great power, penetrating the darkness and giving life to your whole body...making you feel alive, free, energized....***Bring to mind times when you have felt that energy before. What made you feel so alive?***...*(Allow time here for reflection.)*

Focus again on that sparkle of light as it pulsates, bounces, dances within you. Imagine now that other circles of light are being playfully tossed towards you. As you catch each one, the light penetrates your whole person and joins the circle of light in the center. Your own circle increases in size and you feel more and more energized and free. ***Who are people in your life who help you to feel empowered?*** Allow yourself to bathe and soak in that light from others....*(Allow time here.)*

Your circle of light has grown so large, light emanates from you. You are bursting with power. Imagine reaching into the circle, as you would into a quiver for an arrow, and pulling out a circle of light the size of a snowball.

Toss it up in the air and catch it. As you do, it doubles in size. Juggle it for a moment as you think of someone you would like to share it with. When ready, toss it to the person like a beach ball, and when it reaches its goal, it will completely fill the person, shining out with great energy. ***Think of a time when you did something for someone and that person was happier and more whole. How did you feel?***... *(Allow time here.)*

You are never diminished by giving your light away. Instead, it becomes more powerful. Now make an identical ball of light for yourself. Toss it over your head and let it settle around you, over you, through you, until you glow like the person you just blessed. ***What do you do for yourself that empowers you?***... *(Allow time here.)*

Allow this energy to stay with you and carry it with you even when this ritual is over and into tomorrow. When you are ready, open your eyes. Feel your power.

GROUP SHARING:
(Group members can share reactions/reflections to this exercise. Questions from the meditation [marked with ***] can be repeated or written out to facilitate discussion.)

CLOSING THE CIRCLE:
The symbol of empowerment is again passed around the circle. This time it is held high by each woman and silently but reverently passed on to the next woman.

(When all have finished, a song ["Circling Free" by Marsie Sylvestro, from *Circling Free*, Moonsong Productions], or any music or chant can be used to start the clasped hand circle revolving by walking, slowly at first, then moving faster and faster. Or, simply take hands and feel the energy of those present. At the end of the music, clasped hands are raised high as leader proclaims or chants: "The circle is open, but unbroken. Blessed are we." Group repeats.)

CLOSING SONG:
"The Circle Song" by Marsie Sylvestro, from *Crossing the Line*, Moonsong Productions, or "Circle of Love" by Miriam Therese Winter, from *WomanSong* (Medical Mission Sisters, 1987).

Celebration of a Circle of Friends

SYMBOL: Spices

PREPARATION:
   Each person is given a sheet of paper or stationery and a fine-tip color marker (additional colors available in a central space). A coffee cup with ground spices,e.g., cinnamon, allspice, ginger, and nutmeg, is on a small table in celebration circle.

SONG FOR CENTERING:
   (Listen.) "Prayer to Friends" by Carolyn McDade, on *This Tough Spun Web*, Women at Grailville, or "My Friend, You Are a Miracle" by Marsie Sylvestro, on *Circling Free*, Moonsong Productions, or "That's What Friends Are For," Dionne Warwick.

READING 1:   John 15:15-17

READING 2:   "Over a Cup of Coffee" by Marge Sears

Come on over, we'll all sit down—*(All:)* over a cup of coffee.
Haven't seen you for a while—*(All:)* over a cup of coffee.

Let's take some time for us— *(All:)* over a cup of coffee.
We'll let the stories flow—*(All:)* over a cup of coffee.

Even if a few tears spill—*(All:)* over a cup of coffee.
Time is never wasted— *(All:)* over a cup of coffee.
   Because...
We become nourished—*(All:)* over a cup of coffee.

REFLECTION AND EXPRESSION:
(Recall a favorite friendship ritual (like meeting for coffee) or a special memory
of a time spent with a friend[s]. On your paper, draw a picture, write a poem,
or write a letter of gratitude to the friend[s]. [Play "Sister" by Chris Williamson, on *The Changer and the Changed*, Olivia Records, or instrumental music.])

SHARING:
(Anyone who wishes may share her reflections or expressions with the group.)

READING 3:   "Sisters" by Mary Ann D. Carolin

Always present, gently touching,
soothing my troubled heart.
Sharing   time
            ideas
            self
never afraid to enter in with me
the who that I am
            in love
discovering, always becoming,
            my sisters
            my friends
together sacrament.

GRATITUDE CIRCLE:
Let us stand and open our circle to the spirits of those friends we hold in gratitude as we open our hearts to all that they are and all that we are when we are
with them. We invite them here by following this pattern: I love you, *(name)*,
for/because of *(what this friend brings or brings out in your friendship)*. For exam-

ple: "I love you, Sheila, for drawing out into the light all the creativity and good in me that few others looked quite deep enough to find."

ALL:
With hearts of gratitude, we thank you, God/dess, our Eternal Friend, for gifting us with the spicy warmth of good friends.

We are grateful because they have chosen us to be their friends—loving our colors, our fragrance, the essence of who we are.

By the mingling of our friendship, we have come to savor life and love as one flavorful herbal tea which soothes, heals, refreshes, and pleases us as our needs require.

We praise the power of our ever-fresh friendship that expands our happiness and transforms our sorrow.

May it render our hearts open to taste and relish new friendships.

Blessed are you, O God/dess of Unity, for spicing our lives through friendship.

Blessed are we for our potpourri of friends.

BLESSING:
Let us bless one another with these zest-filled spices (*holds up cup*) and may their scents remind us of the sweetness each of our friendships brings. (*The cup is passed around as each says a blessing for the person next to her as she dabs a bit of the spice on the back of her hands.*)

SONG:
(*played during blessing*) "Blessing Song" by Marsie Sylvestro, on *Circling Free*, or "Blessing Song" by Miriam Therese Winter, on *WomanSong*, or "May Your Lives Be Blessed" by Carey Landry, on *Companions on the Journey*, N.A.L.R.

Connecting With the Past
Prophetic Voices of Women

SYMBOL: Voices

SONG:
   "Walk Through These Doors" by Marsie Sylvestro, on *Crossing the Line*, Moon-song Productions, or "Chant of a Wide Terrain, chant 1" by Carolyn McDade, on *Tough Spun Web*, Women at Grailville.

INTRODUCTION:
   In the past, women have been labeled passive. When women spoke, our talk was labeled as idle, silly, chatty, or gossipy. Too often, in the face of injustice, we stood mute in order to be safe. But our silence did not save us. Our children were harmed, our sisters wasted, our earth poisoned, and our selves distorted. We must speak what is most important to us, like the valiant women of the past and present who speak with prophetic voices of change.

READING: "A Herstory of Women's Voices" by Marge Sears

I hear voices through the centuries,
I feel spirit throughout time.
Courageous women who have struggled
Bringing insight to life's rhyme.

Voices, silenced in the textbooks,
Still whispering, shouting through the years.
Ordinary women who have worked
Bringing change by courage and tears.

Voices in politics, education, health care
Crying against the status quo,
Extraordinary women who have challenged
bringing growth despite their foes.

Voices swelling in their volume;
Some wisely wispy, others highly pitched with innocence.
Young women, old women, singly, together
Bringing from past to the present, women's influence.

Voices teaching, singing, preaching;
Speaking out or silently allowing actions say.
Women of all races, creeds
Telling the herstory, we celebrate today.

THE PROPHETIC VOICES OF WOMEN:
(Each section can be read by a different individual. After each section, all respond: "Empower us, prophetic women.")

Miriam—Priest and Prophetess, leader of celebration
Exodus 15: 20-21: "The prophetess Miriam, Aaron's sister, took tambourine in her hand, while all the women went out after her with tambourines dancing, and she led them in the refrain: Sing to the Lord, for he is gloriously triumphant; horse and chariot he has cast into the sea."

Deborah—Prophetess and Judge, leader of the downtrodden
Deborah 4:3-4: "The peasantry ceased in Israel, they ceased until you arose, Deborah, arose as a mother in Israel! Then marched down the remnant of the noble; the people of the Lord marched down for him against the mighty."

Mary Magdalene, Joanna, Mary, and the Other Women—Disciples, Preachers, first to preach the good news
Luke 24: 1, 8-9, 11: "But very early Sunday morning they took ointments to the tomb—and found that the huge stone covering the entrance had been rolled aside. So they went in—but the Lord Jesus' body as gone....Then they remem-

bered and rushed back to Jerusalem to tell his eleven disciples—and everyone else—what had happened. But the story sounded like a fairy tale to the men—they didn't believe it."

Phoebe—Deacon, Priscilla—Evangelizer, leader of early Christian community
Romans 16:1-4: "Phoebe, a dear Christian woman from the town of Cenchreae, will be coming to see you soon. She has worked hard in the church there. Receive her as your sister in the Lord, giving her a warm Christian welcome. Help her in every way you can, for she has helped many in their needs, including me. Tell Priscilla and Aquila hello. They have been my fellow workers in the affairs of Jesus Christ. In fact, they risked their lives for me; and I am not the only one who is thankful to them; so are all Gentile churches."

Julian of Norwich — Mystic, leading us to a fullness of images from *Revelations of Divine Love:*
"Thus Jesus Christ, who does good against evil, is our very Mother. We have our being of him, there, where the ground of Motherhood begins; with all the sweet keeping of love that endlessly follows. As truly as God is our Father, so truly is God our Mother."

MODERN-DAY PROPHETS:

Mother Teresa—prophesying with her work with the outcast and dying.

Ita Ford, Maura Clark, Dorothy Kazel, Jean Donovan—prophesied with their lives and work with the opressed of Central America.

Delores Huerta—prophesying for just wages and humane working conditions for farm workers.

Kateri Tekawitha—prophesied and suffered for the faith incarnated in Native Americans.

Sr. Theresa Kane—prophesied for the suffering of women in the church and called for full participation.

Dorothy Day—prophesied through her writing and her hospitality to the city's poorest. "Show me a man who says the Lord hated blacks, and I'll show you a man with no sense in his head and no love in his heart."

Corazon Aquino—prophesied for an end to dictatorship in the Philippines and modeled for women in political leadership.

SILENCE:
In the silence now, listen for the voices of women in your life who have inspired and influenced you. (*Leave a few minutes of quiet.*)

NAMING OF THE VOICES:
(One after another, in a random fashion, name out loud the voices who have influenced you.)

BLESSING PRAYER:
Spirit of God, you are a life-giving spirit who set us free. Inspire us with courage to claim our voices and proclaim the truth discovered in our own experience. Bless our mouths with prophetic voices. *(Sign your own lips and then those of the people on either side of you.)*

We know that we are not alone, however. Our ancestors and our contemporaries shape our voice, our understanding, our passions. Continue to send your spirit though their prophetic voices that challenge us and energize us. Bless our ears to hear. *(Sign your ears and those of the ones next to you.)*

Send your spirit to make us whole that we may celebrate all that is good and human, and all that is women in us. Bless our womanly bodies. *(Sign yourself and sign those next to you.)* Amen.

SONG:
"Let the Women Be There" by Marsie Sylvestro, on *Crossing the Line*, Moonsong Productions, or "Women" by Miriam Therese Winter, on *WomanSong* (Medical Mission Sisters, 1987), or "Sure As the Wind" by Libana, on *A Circle Is Cast*, Spinning Records.

Connecting With Mother Earth

SYMBOL: Earth

PREPARATION:
Large earthenware bowl is filled with soil. If at all possible, hold ritual out of doors (or place indoors that looks out over the outdoors). Before ritual, practice movements to closing song. Circle is formed standing or sitting on the ground.

CENTERING:
(Music from *Missa Gaia* [Earth Mass], or any Paul Winter album as someone carries the earthenware bowl first around the outside of the circle and then the inside of the circle.)

LEADER:

Since time began, the earth has been looked upon as feminine, a womb from which all life comes and the tomb to which we all return at death. Even in our technologically advanced society, we are still in tune with the earth's rhythms: solar cycle, lunar cycle, and seasons. We eat of her fruits and, on her land, we walk, play, and love. Today, we celebrate our connectedness and dependence on mother earth and on all creation, as we praise our Creator. Let us take time to bring to mind how we have personally experienced the soil.

As the bowl of soil is passed, person to person, reflect as you trace, handle, mold, sift, or play in the earth. Recall your memories with dirt—making mud pies, gardening, molding clay, building sand castles or a home, burying a loved one, or walking barefoot on a beach. *(Play selections from Missa Gaia—e.g., "All the Beauty of the Earth," as bowl is passed.)*

READER 1:

Then God formed a human creature of the dust from the ground and breathed into the creature's nostrils the breath of life.

READER 2:

"Take off your shoes," God said, "The place on which you are standing is holy ground."

READER 3:

"The earth is full of the goodness of God."

READER 4:

"Jesus spit on the ground, made clay with the spittle, put this over the eyes of the blind man and said to him, 'Go and wash.'"

READER 5:

"Jesus bent down and started tracing on the ground with his finger. When he straightened up, he said, 'Let the man among you who has no sin be the first to cast a stone at her.'"

READER 6:

"The one who receives the seed in rich soil is the one who hears the word and understands it."

READER 7:

"For dust you are and to dust you shall return."

READER 8:

"Then I saw a new heaven and a new earth."

SHARING:

The women are invited to share their memories with soil or their reflections on the previously read Scripture passages and what connections they have made with both.

READING:

Native Americans have always had a profound respect and reverence for the earth and for all of creation. The following is from a speech given by an angry chief before being forced to sign away the land in 1855.

"I Wonder If the Ground Has Anything to Say" by Lawrence Kip, The Indian Council In the Valley of Walla Walla

I wonder if the ground has anything to say? I wonder if the ground is listening to what is said? I wonder if the ground will come alive and what is on it? The ground says, It is the Great Spirit that placed me here. The Great Spirit tells me to take care of the Indians, to feed them right. The Great Spirit appointed the roots to feed Indians on. The water says the same thing.

The Great Spirit directs me, Feed the Indians well. The grass says the same thing, Feed the Indians well. The ground, water, and grass say, The Great Spirit has given us our names. We have these names and hold these names.

The ground says, The Great Spirit has placed me here to produce all that grows on me, trees and fruits. The same way the ground says, It was from me man was made. The Great Spirit, in placing people on the earth, desired them to take good care of the ground and to do each other no harm....

PRAYER:

A section of "Prayer of the Four Directions," a Native American ritual
(People bend or squat to touch the earth.)

We celebrate you, Great Mother Earth, placed here by the Creator. From you we came and you feed us still and continue to provide us with shelter.

Teach us to respect your lands, to care for your gifts, and to share cooperatively with our brothers and sisters of all creation.

Some day, we will return to you and to our Creator as a child returns to the warm embrace of her mother, enfolded in her loving arms.

All praise to you, O Mother Earth, who enables us to find our Creator in the gifts of all creation.

CLOSING SONG:
(with optional ritual movements) "Mother Earth" by Miriam Therese Winter, on *WomanSong*, (Medical Mission Sisters, 1987).

(Form standing circle.)

Chorus:
Mother Earth *(Arms move down sides to touch ground, then each other to form circle that comes up over head.)*
Sister Sea *(Circle broken, arms straight out at shoulder level, moving in wavelike motions.)*
Giving birth *(Arms down to meet and cup below waist, then bring cupped hands extended forward.)*
Energy *(Hands separate, both then spiral upwards above head.)*
Reaching out *(Arms go straight out at shoulder level, touching hands of persons next to you.)*
Touching Me *(Hands come in to touch cheeks.)*
Lovingly *(Arms cross in front of chest as if to hug.)*

(Verse can be read out loud as song is sung on tape. People can be still during verses or move spontaneously, coming together for movement during each chorus.)

ALTERNATIVE CLOSING:
Play Native American music (available at most public libraries), or "Mother Earth" by Libana, on *A Circle Is Cast*, Spinning Records.

Connecting Globally

SYMBOLS: Ethnic breads, Wine

PREPARATION:
Different participants are asked to bake or bring the different types of ethnic bread found in the ritual below. Readers for the dramatic reading should be selected ahead of time to allow for practice and to ensure its fullest impact. Goblet of wine (or grape juice) is placed at or on table of celebration.

INTRODUCTION:
We have only to watch an evening news program to hear of the divisions and conflicts in our world: Irish/English, Iraq/Iran, South African white/black, peasant/landowner, rich/poor, etc. What we hear less of are those who work for peace and who strive to make connections globally. Let us center ourselves as we listen to this song about making connections.

SONG:
"Song of Solidarity" by Carolyn McDade, on *Tough Spun Web*, Women at Grailville, or "Call to Women" by Carolyn McDade, on *We Come With Our Voices*, Women at Grailville, or "Weary Mothers of the Earth" by Joan Baez, on *Come From the Shadow*, A & M Records.

DRAMATIC READING:
"Rich Woman/Poor Woman," reading for two women dressed for their respective parts. Anonymous

1. I am a woman.

2. I am a woman born of woman, whose man owned a factory.

3. I am a woman whose man wore silk suits, who constantly watched his weight.

4. I am a woman who watched two babies grow into beautiful children.

5. I am a woman who watched twins grow into popular college students with summers abroad.

6. But then there was a man,

7. and he talked about the peasants getting richer by my family getting poorer.

8. We had to eat rice!

9. We had to eat beans!

10. My children were no longer given summer visas to Europe,

11. And I felt like a peasant,

12. a peasant with a dull, hard, unexciting life,

1. I am a woman.

2. I am a woman born of a woman, whose man labored in a factory.

3. I am a woman whose man wore tattered clothing, whose heart was constantly strangled by hunger.

4. I am a woman who watched two babies die because there was no milk.

5. I am a woman who watched three children grow, with bellies stretched from no food.

6. But then there was a man,

7. and he told me of days that would be better, and he made the days better.

8. We ate rice.

9. We had beans.

10. My children no longer cried themselves to sleep.

11. And I felt like a woman,

12. like a woman with a life that sometimes allowed a song.

13. And I saw a man,

14. and together we began to plot with the hope of the return of freedom...

15. Someday, the return to freedom.

16. And then,

17. one day,

18. there were planes overhead and guns firing close by.

19. I gathered my children and went home,

20. and the guns moved farther and farther away.

21. And then they announced that freedom had been restored!

22. They came into my home along with my man,

23. Those men whose money was almost gone...

24. And we had drinks to celebrate,

25. the most wonderful martinis.

26. And they asked us to dance,

27. me,

28. and my sisters.

29. And then they took us.

13. And I saw a man.

14. I saw his heart begin to beat with the hope of freedom at last...

15. Someday, freedom.

16. But then,

17. one day,

18. there were planes overhead and guns firing in the distance.

19. I gathered my children and ran,

20. but the guns moved closer and closer.

21. And then they came, young boys really...

22. They came and found my man.

23. They found all of the men whose lives were almost their own,

24. and they shot them all.

25. They shot my man.

26. And they came for us,

27. for me, the woman,

28. for my sisters.

29. Then they took us.

30. They took us to dinner at a small private club,

31. and they treated us to beef.

32. It was one course after another.

33. We nearly burst, we were so full.

34. It was magnificent to be free again!

35. And then they gathered the children together...

36. And he gave them some good wine...

37. And then we gave them a party.

38. The beans have disappeared now.

39. The rice: I've replaced it with chicken or steak.

40. And the parties continue, night after night, to make up for all the time wasted.

41. And I feel like a woman again.

30. They stripped from us the dignity that we had gained,

31. and they raped us.

32. One after another they came at us,

33. lunging, plunging...sisters bleeding, sisters dying.

34. It was hardly a relief to have survived.

35. And they took our children...

36. and they took their scissors...

37. and then they took the hands of our children...(*Pause*)

38. The beans have disappeared.

39. The rice, I cannot find it.

40. And my silent tears are joined once more by the midnight cries of my children.

41. They say, I am a woman.

REFLECTION:

Where do you see yourself in the story? What part of the story calls up strong feelings? What are they? What can we do to change the scenario of hunger and desperation presented here?

SONG:

"Cry of the Poor" by John Foley, S.J., on *Wood Hath Hope*, N.A.L.R, or "Bread for the Hungry" by Joe Wise, on *Songs for the Journey*, Pastoral Arts Associates of North America.

BREAD RITUAL:

O God of Unity from Diversity, just as one single woman cannot represent the world, one loaf of bread cannot feed the world's hungry. We bless many kinds of bread today to connect our hungers with the hungers of women throughout the world who suffer, endure, learn, prophesy, and work for peace and unity. *(All place outstretched hand over breads.)* We bless this bread as a sign of nourishment and survival that will give us energy to do good works and to strengthen the bonds of women throughout the world.

(Each woman presents her bread as it appears below, then starts it around the circle for all to share. Use as many languages as possible and add or change varieties of bread according to the background of your group.)

I bring rice cakes to this table. In ancient times, rice was kept for medicinal purposes. Let these rice cakes stand for those who are ill and those who work to prevent or heal illnesses. Let it connect us to the women from the Orient.

I bring unleavened bread to this table. This bread calls to mind refugees, like the Jews of old, who had to leave homes and homelands. Let it connect us to the women of the Middle East.

I bring tortillas to this table, which brings to mind the conflicts in Central America, those who suffer from war and those who make peace. Let this bread connect us with women from Latin America.

I bring rye bread to this table. This bread was the staple for the working class throughout Europe. Let it stand for women who work, who are unemployed, and who are discriminated against in employment. Let this bread connect us with women from European backgrounds.

I bring cornbread to this table. This bread, a regional specialty of the South, represents black people of African and Caribbean background who still suffer from discrimination and injustice. Let this bread connect with women of color throughout the world.

I bring shortbread to this table. Shortbread brings to mind children, the future of our world. Let this bread connect us with our little sisters throughout the world, so that someday this world will be a better place.

SHARING OF WINE (GRAPE JUICE):

Good and Loving God/dess, you who create the fruit of the vine to lighten our hearts, we know that we are not a perfect world and must drink both from the cup of suffering and gladness. We toast our lives and our future in solidarity with all women of the world. *(Cup is raised and then shared.)*

SONG:

"Nosotras venceremos," traditional melody, "We Shall Overcome" by Carolyn McDade, on *Tough Spun Web*, Women at Grailville, or "E Ya Ho Ujaman" (We Are Unity), same as above, or "Companions on the Journey" by Carey Landry, on *Companions on the Journey*, N.A.L.R, or "One Bread, One Body" by John Foley, S.J., on *Wood Hath Hope*, N.A.L.R.

References and Resources

Baez, Joan. *Come From the Shadows*, published by A & M Records.

Bierhorst, John. *Four Masterworks of American Indian Literature*. New York: Farrar, Straus and Giroux, 1974.

Cunningham, Nancy Brady. *Feeding the Spirit* (ritual sourcebook). Resource Publications, 160 E. Virginia St., # 290, San Jose, CA 95112, 1988.

Deitering, Carolyn. *Actions, Gestures, and Bodily Actions*. Resource Publications, 160 E. Virginia St., #290, San Jose, CA 95112, 1980.

Demetrakopoulos, Stephanie. *Listening to Our Bodies*. Boston: Beacon Press, 1983, from Unitarian Universalist Association of Congregations in North America, 25 Beacon St., Boston, MA 02116.

Dufford, Bob. *Earthen Vessels*, produced by N.A.L.R., 10802 N. 23rd Ave., Phoenix, AZ 85029.

Foley, John. *Wood Hath Hope*, produced by N.A.L.R., 10802 N. 23rd Ave., Phoenix, AZ 85029.

Gjerding, Iben and Katherine Kinnamon. *Women's Prayer Services*. Twenty-Third Publications, P.O. Box 180, Mystic, CT. 1983.

Halpin, Marlene. *Imagine That: Using Phantasy in Spiritual Direction*. Iowa: Wm. Brown Co., 1982.

Haugen, Marty. *Night of Silence*. G.I.A. Publications, 7404 South Mason Ave., Chicago, IL 60638.

Hayes, Edward. *Prayers for the Domestic Church*. Forest of Peace Books, Inc., Route 1, Box 247, Easton, KS 66020, 1979.

Iglehart, Hallie. *Womanspirit: A Guide to Women's Wisdom*. New York: Harper & Row, 1983.

Koontz, Christian. *Connecting Creativity and Spirituality*., Kansas City, MO: Sheed & Ward, 1986.

Kozak, Pat, and Janet Schaffran. *More Than Words*., Chicago: Meyer Stone, 1986

Ladyslipper Catalog and Resource Guide (records, tapes, videos by women). P.O. Box 3130, Durham, NC 27705.

Landry, Carey. Various albums published by N.A.L.R., 10802 N. 23rd Ave., Phoenix, AZ 85029.

Lawrence, Kip. The Indian Council in the Valley of the Walla Walla, 1855.

Libana. *A Circle Is Cast,* produced by Spinning Records, P.O. Box 530, Cambridge, MA 02140.

McDade, Carolyn. *We Come With Our Voices. This Tough Spun Web.* Surtsey Publishing. Order from Womancenter at Plainville, 76 Everett Skinner Rd., Plainville, MA 02762.

Meditations With ... series (Hildegard, Julian, Mechtild, Native Americans, Meister Eckhart). Bear and Co., P.O. Drawer 2860, Santa Fe, NM 87504.

National Council of the Churches of Christ in the USA. *An Inclusive Language Lectionary.* Readings for cycles A, B, C. Order from Division of Education and Ministry, NCCC, Room 704, 475 Riverside Drive, New York, NY 10115-0050.

Near, Holly. Music produced by Redwood Records, 476 West MacArthur Blvd., Oakland, CA 94609.

Neu, Diann. *Women Church Celebrations.* Resource from WATER, Silver Spring, MD 20910.

Ruether, Rosemary Radford. *Women-Church.* New York: Harper & Row, 10 East 53rd St., New York, NY. 1985.

Schutte, Dan. *Neither Silver or Gold,* produced by N.A.L.R., 10802 N. 23rd Ave., Phoenix, AZ 85029.

Sweet Honey in the Rock. Produced by Flying Fish Records, 4304 West Schubert, Chicago, IL 60614.

Sylvestro, Marsie. *Circling Free* and *Crossing the Line* by Moonsong Productions, 17 Ames St. #3, Sommerville MA 02145.

Williamson, Chris. *The Changer and the Changed,* produced by Olivia Records, Inc., 4400 Market St., Oakland, CA 94608.

Winston, George. *Autumn. December.* Windham Hill Records, Box 9588, Stanford, CA 94305.

Winter, Miriam Therese. *WomanPrayer, WomanSong: Resources for Ritual*. Book, Meyer Stone Books, 1987. Album, order from Medical Mission Sisters, 77 Sherman St., Hartford, CT 06105.

Winter, Paul. *Missa Gaia*, by Living Music Records, P.O. Box 72, Litchfield, CT 06759.

Wise, Joe. *Songs for the Journey*. Pastoral Arts Associates of North America, 4744 W. Country Gables, Glendale, CA 95306.

Wuellner, Flora Slosson. *Prayer and Our Bodies*. Upper Room, 1908 Grand Ave., P.O. Box 189, Nashville, TN 37202, 1987.

Wynne, Patricia. *The Womanspirit Sourcebook*. New York: Harper & Row, 1988.